Elizabeth Royal Patton Poetry Prize Anthology

2024

Elizabeth Royal Patton Poetry Prize Anthology

2024

Clara Songbirds
Publishing House

Clare Songbirds Publishing House Poetry Series
ISBN 978-1-957221-19-9

© 2024 Clare Songbirds Publishing House

Edited by Laura Williams French

Printed in the United States of America
FIRST EDITION

140 Cottage Street
Auburn, New York 13021
www.claresongbirdspub.com

Contents

First Prize
Kathleen Strafford—*The Almanac of Last Things*
1

Second Prize
Sheila Dietz—*Foundation Stone*
2

Third Prize
Kathleen Romano—*Desiderium*
3

Honorable Mention
Ron Carey—*Inchydoney*
4

Long and Short-Listed Poems
*(in alphabetical order: * indicates short list)*

Mary Anne Abdo
—*Artificial Intelligence*   6

Logan Anthony
—*circular narrative pt. 2*   7

Lorraine Bruno Arsenault
—*This Side of Grass*   8
— *The Witching Hour*   10

Ben Bruges
—*Driving Memories*   11

Ron Carey
—*The Burning of the Books*   12
—*On Writing a Poem on the Love Life of
    Walt Whitman ...*   13

Debra Cartwright
—*Sapience*   14
—*Ode to O'*   15
—*Open Door*   16

Max Chmielewski
   —The Bull   17

Sheila Dietz
   — Reassuring Fire   18
   *— *Boy on a Bicycle*   19

Stacie Eirich
   —April, in the After   20
   — Peeling the Orange: Notes on Bach's Cello Suite   21
   — Second Line   22

Janet Fagal
   *—*Tea for All the Broken Places*   23
   *— *Beach Music*   24

Deborah Filanowski
   —Maybe I Can Start with a Tattoo   25
   — All Good Fairy Tales End in Blood   26
   — In Whom Can We Trust?   28

Mary Gardner
   —Between Times   29
   — On the Issue of Provenance   30
   *— *The Great Tsunami, December 26, 2004*   31

Caitlin Gemmel
   —Bloodlines   33
   —In Memory of Steven Hens   34

Carol Lynn Stevenson Grellas
   *—*Trying to Remember the Unforgettable*   35

Elizabeth Hayhoe
   *—*Rose Coloured Glasses*   36

John Herington
   —Paper Pretzels   38
   —Apotheosis   39

Lindsey Jacobs
   —How to Write a Poem in Ten Steps   40
   *—*A Body is Water*   42
   —Daedalus Grieves   43

Jennifer Maloney
—*Dear Orgasm   44
—*Glass   46
—Unspeakable   48

Katherine Meadows
—*Compendium of Sunlights   50

Nicole Metts
—Passing   53
—A Mother Wars   54
—*Ophelia   55

Kate Potter
—Out There   56
—Nursing Home   57

Mohammed Shohidur Rahman
—A Spider's Love for Cheryl   58

Lynne Schmidt
—When I Run Out of Things to Talk About, I Talk
    About Horses   60
—*The Wedding Ring   61

Peggy Seely
—Home   62
—Spacebar Skips   63
—Comforter   64

Kathleen Strafford
—Family Reunion   65
—*On the Farm with the Warren Boys   66

Bill Tope
—I Have Dreams, Too   67

Luke Williams
—The Extra Mile   69

Diana Woodcock
—To Live in the Grace of Gaia   70

Elizabeth Royal Patton
April 18, 1935– August 20, 2021

The Elizabeth Royal Patton Poetry Prize is named after an early supporter of Clare Songbirds Publishing House. Born and educated in the South, Elizabeth Patton lived in New York for most of her adult life where she taught English at Skaneateles High School. Patton's writing appeared in a variety of journals, literary magazines, anthologies, and newspapers. While Elizabeth wrote in many genres she is best remembered for her poetry and short stories. She published three chapbooks of poetry, *Late Harvest* (Pudding House), *Autumn Notes* (DownTown Books), and *Seasons of the Mind,* which was one of the first books published by Clare Songbirds in 2017. She also wrote a collection of short stories about growing up in the south titled *Feeling for Eggs* posthumously published by Clare Songbirds in 2023.

Patton's support was instrumental in the foundation of Clare Songbirds. Her faith in the fledgling company was rooted in her relationship with Co-founder Heidi Nightengale. Both Nightengale and associate editor Rachael Ikins were among Patton's students in Skaneateles. Patton remained in contact with them long after graduation and supported their writing endeavors throughout her life, often attending readings or offering critique. Her standing as an established writer and belief in Clare Songbird's mission to provide a print forum for fine art from poets and writers lent credibility to the nascent publishing house.

Patton was known for her wit and humor which was reflected in much of her writing. Her blend of southern charm and northern sass combined to produce earnest and eloquent poetry that could induce belly laughs or provoke intense discussion.

With the creation of the *Elizabeth Royal Patton Poetry Prize*, we hope to both honor the memory of a poet and educator who was so instrumental in the success of the publishing house and inspire the next generation of poets. In this inaugural edition of the competition, we received submissions from more than a dozen states, Canada, Ireland, United Kingdom, and South Africa. We were astonished at the quality of the submitted work and are proud to share some of these works with you.

Laura Williams French, editor

Elizabeth Royal Patton

Night Leaves

I used to read about the twelve princesses
who wandered off at night to dance, wearing
out their slippers and perplexing their father.

I was there with them, walking through the tunnel
and coming out under trees of silver and gold,
watching them dance, invisible like the prince
who solved the mystery, and then returning,
my hands cradling a few leaves, memorizing seams.

I still feel close to leaves, waiting for them
to drop, raking them, and wading through drifts.
When I think of going, I think of night,
invisible, touching the leaves, knowing
our surfaces and our destinations.

Night Leaves originally appeared in Yankee Magazine

The Almanac of Last Things
After Linda Paston

I choose the bumble bee buzzing on the floor
hoping for a taste of honey
to fly again
              if only for a day

I choose the Song of Solomon
              its juicy pomegranate perfume
                            dripping between breasts
the young stag charged by gazelles
leaping to where love is a spontaneous fountain

I choose the knocking undertaker
his sunken cheeks and shiny shoes
              holding a measuring tape
                            pennies for eyes

I choose glimmering December
              with its icy-frost mornings
until the garish sun steals the show
And the full moon small enough to fit in my pocket
to save until darkness swells

I choose you over and over
              & your hundred small delights
                            burning with ideas
                                          that make my heart race
The winter light is cold
              & your body is my stove

Foundation Stone

Today, out walking, I came across
  a lichen-encrusted foundation-stone
    chiseled almost 200 years ago

with letters HD and rough numbers. Once
  a quarried granite setting stone anchoring
    a home, now tossed into a ragged line

of mismatched fieldstones—dislodged remnant of an old
  house, like so many we left behind with one move after
    another, homes I long to reinhabit in my dreams. Nightly

I conjure suitcases, pack up my belongings and leave because
  the new owners of these nocturnal houses won't let me
    stay and I am tossed like this cornerstone, landing

in a memory of my father when he would drive the four of us
  to the nearest woods where he urged us to collect
    rocks he'd later toss into the backyard stream flowing

past our forever home, the one we lived in longest, while these stones
  I pass daily only hope to stop a car that's careened off the road
    into sorrow I can't shake, though one day

I did see a garden snake curled on the flat top of the foundation stone
  warming in sun. And today, I startled a mouse to scurry
    between rocks while a bee nuzzled a pink peony

nestled in clusters of creeping buttercup. I still long to return
  the foundation stone to its true home though I know
    the house anchored

is, like me, scattered and detached even as I can see nearby
  tendrils from twining wisteria
    cast about the air for purchase.

Kathleen Romano
Third Prize

Desiderium

I missed my brother by nineteen months, our lives a set of parallel lines destined never to cross. His once larger than life presence, dwarfed only by the gaping hole of his absence, clung resolutely to every inch of the house long after he was carried out of it. Clothes, letters, and cassette tapes packed neatly into a box were all that remained. I'd bury my face in a shirt and imagine I could faintly catch his scent through the dust of decades. I'd think I knew him for a moment. I'd pour over every inch of that box, hoping each time to find something I'd missed. Something he'd left for me that would have somehow sustained me for this life without him. Something so I wouldn't have to imagine him in songs he never heard and jokes we never shared. If I sit still for long enough, he comes and sits in a chair he never sat in, and we have conversations we'll never have. His voice sounds like the soft rain hitting the window. I'll hold his hand I've never touched, and it's warm. Grief's imagination, I've found, is very like a sparrow who upon losing her nest finds another and convinces herself the eggs inside are her own.

Ron Carey
Honorable Mention

Inchydoney

Here, on the light-skinned beach at Inchydoney, with the tide
So far out it looks like it might never return, even
If you don't believe in God you must admit
Someone is really good on the details.
Take that cormorant sweeping the waves, head
Tilted towards a sky of mirrors, with all its skim
And swiftness lowered, almost cresting, almost touching.
And now another, following the same path, a path invisible
To the eye, spun in colour and the power of flight.
And down they come, holding their wings out to dry
In September's fast fading.
I think they must be a pair, see how they bend their question
Shaped heads, too close to be anything but lovers.
Though your hand has been in mine all day, I suddenly feel it,
Warm and wonderfully alive, like a small bird in its nest.

Long & Short-listed
Poems by Author

Mary Anne Abdo

Artificial Intelligence

I don't want a computer
to write the words,
that need to be heard.
Intimate thoughts,
and words that come from this feeble mind.
I want these conceptualizations,
these feelings,
to be naturally mine.
Hearing cues from my grandmother,
look up spelling words in a dictionary.
Use your own mind.
Wanting all of my words to be,
my own style,
my poetic language.
I will not step,
and fetch with modernity.
Intellect is sacred.
Writing for the world,
is an inward process,
to portray outwardly to humanity's stage
Linguistics is a skill of natural beauty.
I want to have this human intrinsic dialog,
with every color of this blessed earth.
That only humanity can conjure,
letters to words,
word to sentences,
inventing paragraphs of explosive
odysseys of paradise lost.
It is a revolution,
it is a revelation,
it is a never ending cerebrum of electricity,
it is laughing,
it is crying,
it is screaming,
it is loving,
it is human gift,
that is to behold.

circular narrative pt. 2

… july. it's been august. september has almost gone. still.
i crave to see your hands sitting folded
in your lap, to hear your voice that circles like a dog before it
settles at my feet. when this season has passed, i wonder
at your whereabouts. i wonder at the flavors you taste. the spark
you ignite behind you,
blazing your way through. i wonder at the thoughts like
raindrops stippling the surface of your mind. raindrops i used to
drink from your cupped hands, when you'd let me. the time is
running as always, gaining on me. ruthless even with its mercy.
teeth sink into the soft flesh at the backs of my legs. flesh and
muscle, blood and bone. these tissues
i leave behind. still running, the jaws tighten around my mid-
section, now. organs will puncture, rupture, and falter. the oper-
ation my body runs will come swiftly to a close. the noose
of the remaining days tightens. fraying rope knotted together.
the burn of rope pulled taut across the skin. we know of this,
here. burning has become a synonym
for too many things. and it's been…

Lorraine Bruno Arsenault

This Side of Grass

A year rolled by, dropped off the horizon,
our last supper together
the one when magnums bled red bouquets.

I bear a bottle.

"Hold the merlot," I hear "ginger ale, please."
The jangle of capsules in your pocket distracts me.
"Oh, sorry," you say, "they keep my drummer beating."

We open mermaid holograms of bodies undulating
in turquoise frames heedless of the star searing.
Their faces nod like bells chiming in wind.

That was us.

A rumble growls from thunderheads.
I give you iced ginger ale,
frosty rills slink from the glass into your hands.

You stare too long at cut flowers.

You say, "remember the Saturday Night Ladies,
who met at The Pier to feast on lobster and wine?"
You titter, "and named the barkeep, Father John?"

"Yes?" I smiled, "I remember."

"Two died. The other doesn't know her children."
Those words topple from you, bounce onto tiles,
fracture into shards I can't seem to gather whole.

I think about this after you leave.

I walk to the beach, amble by umbrella rainbows,
watch sand fleas burrow beneath my footfall along tide's highmark,
the grit of shelldust building between my toes.

It clings still.

I grab for a wave trying to stop it from recoiling to sea,
fumble to entwine sunfingers teasing its crest,
reach for starfish and sand dollars riding its wake.

It's no use.

Palms fill with froth and sand,
seatrophies roll home in a watertrough of exoskeletons
skimming the shore, vanishing in a brew of surf.

The Witching Hour

At 4:30 a.m. there is no light,
only the ink of one's footsteps.

Stars sleep behind branches, in the
shadows of hills,
in lamps peeking out from windows.

Aged oaks tower where mushrooms lift from earth,
where I search for you, for me
under lichens, in the flesh of trees

I slip on wet leaves,
float on magic carpetwords
drift from an aperture of blurred dreams.

Images transform, condense, stretch out,
reflect from fun house mirrors,
tumble around children,

plummet onto colored spaces of maps,
roads void of signs,
bloodrivers seeping into earth.

Unembodied voices perch in an ear,
a draft escapes the flap of wings
a veil flutters.

At 4:30 a.m. there is no light,
there is only hope.

Ben Bruges

Driving memories

The jam stops us where the bank drops away
into a marsh of fallen tree trunks over flat water.

Ivy flower fists, dogwood and yellow flag iris flash
and, for the moment, I'm more there than here,

a break from the rushing blacktop and white lines.
Ravel's string quartet plays whole-tone melodies

while I've been driving dear sleepy passengers

back home after a break from jobs and routine

along this fast A-road all too often closed
by landslide, floods, works and collisions.

An app guides me in twists around tree roots
and ownership disputes. The road is familiar, traced.

The glimpse glides into memory, lasting long enough
to carry away something pure, unused, marginal.

Ron Carey

The Burning of the Books

She left her religion in our care.
Her old prayerbooks and Bible, lapped by mould
And intoxicated by time.
Immediately, we felt the flutter of her anxiety.
We all agreed, the books were too far gone.
Their words tumbling to the floor, detached
From their sacredness.
As we piled them high in the hearth,
I was vaguely aware of something wrong, remembering,
I suppose, old tales of hate against all books,
When even thoughts were set on fire.
It was many days before I put a match to them.
And even then I wasn't sure.
As the blaze took hold of the Bible, something small
And worm-like-wriggled from between the pages of Genesis
And the illiterate flames roared with unthinking joy
As they burned the beautiful, perfumed trees of Eden.

On Writing a Poem on the Love Life of Walt Whitman
Outside the Changing Rooms at Marks and Spencer

The black bears roll between summer skirts and sandals.

The deer are rutting in a forest of jeans, manifestly horned.

The women, natural, good-humoured, patient, flagged

In multi-coloured choices—ignore, at the changing door,

The candour of my waiting.

Far off, under the sparkling eyes of war, I hear the boys

In blue and grey go marching, down the third floor,

Air-conditioned, corridors of splendour.

The Wound Dresser bends to kiss the forehead of a dying soldier,

And all that is human in me fills with tenderness.

I keep writing but I am distracted by the affable assistant.

Her bubbly personality retails confidence to young and old alike.

Her mind rejects all that is negative.

My wife emerges empty handed and unsatisfied.

As we ride the escalator down to Parking, its rattle reminds me

Of that winter night when Walt found love on a Washington tram.

We drive out into the sunlight of a Dublin suburb.

Beyond the settled houses, buffalo cover the plains in shadow.

Debra Cartwright

Sapience

Once upon an ocean shore
I walked until I thought no more,
somewhere along the pebbled beach
I found myself just beyond my reach.

Within a forest dark and deep
I walked until I fell asleep,
mesmerized by the shadowy dance
I lost myself in a dreamer's trance.

High upon a mountain slope
I walked until my heart was broke,
my hopes and dreams all fell away
like characters in a masked parade.

Upon this magic carpet ride
I laughed until the illusion died
and only then did I realize
all is I in disguise.

Ode to O'

O' wee isle in the Northern Sea
Land o' the Shamrock, my ancestry;
"school of the West, quiet be
the habitation o' literature and sanctity."

In dark, silent sanctums o' old
on native tongues our tales unfold
o'er hill, o'er dale to taverns cold
songs o' our ancestors, Kelly green mold.

The half-said thing, bards preferred
our heritage, in Gaelic remains unheard.
Haney; O'Hannaidh tartan unfurled
Oh what the O' imparts to the world.

Open Door

Well-worn shoes on a dusty floor
laying by an open door.
Time slipped by as I paused to stare
and wonder at their reason there.
Forgotten, abandoned and out of place
an image arose of their owner's face.
Turning as I heard a silent tear
slide down a face showing decades of wear.
Eyes spoke an unspoken plea
in a rare moment of mental clarity.
"Help me find usefulness in this aging me."
I touched his cheek and held his hand.
I whispered, "Aging has made you no less of a man.
You are now and have always been,
the love of my life, more so now than then.
I would not trade this time to be
our young at heart carefree selves again."
Noticing the simple things
out of place and usually unseen
opens connections hidden deep
within Love's journey as we mortals sleep.
Shoes left by an open door,
opened a door to so much more.

Max Chmielewski

The Bull

You broke another plate today.
I watched it slip through your fingers and shatter on the ground.
You kept talking, as though you didn't notice its absence,
Didn't hear the crash or see the shards of porcelain on the floor.
I swept the pieces up and hid them away.
How many times have we played this game?

At first, the china cabinet was full of promise,
Ready to be filled with cups and plates and curios;
All in anticipation of dinners, of teas,
Of conversations over emptied plates, long into the night.
We filled it together:
You, with heirlooms and expectations;
Me, with new treasures and hope.
It could have been a beautiful chaos,
Two unlike souls finding common ground.

I know that wasn't what you wanted,
That order and unity were what you sought.
I learned it through empty shelves,
Through broken figures,
Through the smash of ceramic behind your words.
It was always an accident.
You never meant to do it.
I played along and believed you,
Picked up what remained and stored it away:
Another piece of me you didn't want;
Another piece of me I had to hide.

Sometimes I dream of ripping the cabinet away from the wall,
Of hurling it to the floor and shattering everything inside.
Better to do it all at once
Than to linger in this charade.

Sometimes I dream of repairing each piece,
Mending cracks with gold; strength from brokenness.
I'd put everything back where it belonged,
My whole self on display.

If I did, could I trust you not to break it again?

Sheila Dietz

Reassuring Fire

Before the people next door switched
on their lamp, we lounged on the porch,
drinking whisky, laughing
and then talking politics,
shaking our heads in bewilderment
until we notice it's grown quiet
and darker.

The neighbor's lamp now glows
through gauzy curtains. I imagine
the lampshade as faded, perhaps
even slightly stained, while the light itself
strikes me as a strong, steady, and reliable
friend. I picture it radiating warmth
just like this, every night.

I know. Not everyone has a lamp
or a window for the soft light
to fall through. Maybe this soothing
light will come from a campfire, a rusty
streetlight brightening a dangerous street,
or headlights that flicker through trees,

announcing the return of a loved one—
even moonlight reflecting
off a sun-bleached animal bone in the desert
might be a beacon for some lost traveler,
and maybe you or someone you know
will find such a light
banked like a reassuring fire
deep in the eyes of a neighbor,
or the liberating eyes of a friend.

Boy on a Bicycle

The boy rides down a dirt road, jumps his bike
over deep ruts worn by lumbering carts

weighted down with winter rye. Air swells,
redolent of seaweed, salt, waves hissing

just over the tawny horizon. The boy's
hair riffles as he speeds a stone studded road

into town, past his father who, bending,
grabs a handful of powdery earth so fine

it coats the inside of his nose, his hair.
He frowns as the boy rides by kicking

up dust, calls him back. He has something
to say about cover fields of rye, rain

that won't fall from a cloudless blue stretching
lazily above with no sense of urgency,

sky that lured the boy from his house and drove
the farmer to walk his land, lower his troubled

gaze into rain barrels. The boy leans forward,
speeds up, heedless of the sea's allure, church bells

peeling, his name in the salty air. Something
propels him down this road, pedaling

steadily past drooping fields of rye, past
wild daisies loosening their petals into the air.

Stacie Eirich

April, in the after

A month of spring's display, of sun and rain,
color and blooms and branches filled with green.
A month of birthdays and 6-months cancer-free
celebrations and a national recognition of verses.
A month of promenades and music, breath and life multiplied,
earthy and bright and singing — alive. In Aprils past
we painted and sang and read in the sun: planted, biked, baked.
Why, now, do we feel a lack of color and light: a sorrow
wide and gray, stretching across the days, the hours?
The weight of it heavy as rainstorms, a muddy sinking swamp.
The burdens of what may come, what has come, what remains
in the after — after we rise from pediatric cancer's wreckage, if only
to find our way through grief, to recover from loss after loss.
What remains to stand in the light, and who stands beside us?
We can't seem to shake this hole, this chasm consuming
the thread that bound us through treatment, the force of energy
that kept us going. That kept us believing in the better after,
in a world that would welcome and understand us, enfold
and befriend us. Instead, the better after isn't what we imagined.
It is complex and muddied and full of a nagging sadness, a cacophony
of pouring rain with each next loss: of dreams, of memories, of skills,
of security, of safe spaces, of friends, of friendships, of what is
or once was home, of belonging, of who we once were. The fallout
of the after is real and lonely, it hangs in the air both silent and loud,
an emptiness, a hollowness that isn't filled by the sun or the blooms,
the green or the birdsong or a lilting spring breeze. Instead, all this
loveliness pulls a shadow over us,
leaves our pens sometimes silent, our voices paused.
How can we press through to the tenderness that breaks us open,
the beauty and wonder and warmth, the light
that binds us into hopefulness? Into newness,
into something that splinters, then mends into a space of true healing —
one that allows curiosity and connection,
laughter and honest conversation,
something that might make us ready to step back into life? Feet bare
in wet grass, toes squelched in mud, faces flooded in sunlight, eyes up,
breath to blue sky, hearts re-connected to enchantment,
to what is real and what is possible,
to wonder, to a sense of ourselves and the world: embraced, whole.

Peeling the Orange: Notes on Bach's Cello Suite

How is it that Bach lays us bare, unfurls that
which has coiled inside? Listen to the Cello's
harmony, to its taut strings speak
an invitation to prayer.

There is an awe electric in the air, rising
as the fervent bow plays. How is it we come to stillness
as rhythm intensifies? Not exploding but increasing
as if climbing a mountain, gaining in spectacle as it ascends.

If at the piece's final note we are arisen to grace, to something
like holiness: What is it we feel in the silence
that follows? In the moment we are still in the world
but not of the world, in that hushed space.

A sacred space reserved for that which touches us, changes
us. Brings us deeper into the nature of things, into a breath that carries
farther, echoing further than our feet, chords continuing on
through the trees, the sound and soundlessness of space.

The instruments, the composition, the sound, the memory
of sound, the trees, the light eclipsing us. The moment
when music rises us to grace: the peeling of orange, grass
at our feet, wet coolness of mist, beating warmth of sun on skin.

A shedding of skins, of laughter, a tasting
of citrus, an emptying: of tears, of grief, of joy.

Second Line

We feel wisps of breeze, shock of sun, listen to the coo and giggle
of a parent and child playing beyond the fence next door.

We watch the leaves and branches rustle & sway, observe how
the cats care for each other, licking each other's fur and lying at
our feet.

The day bright and warm, a lush-ness falling over the greening
grass, a vibrant hum alive in the air. We try to press past the
sorrow

creeping up inside, catch the light that spins so brilliant, its music
as bright as a brass band, summer sliding in like a trombone in
a second line.

We try to grasp onto the steps of its dance, the rhythm of rays
and birdsong brushing against our sadness. It pulls us from our
chairs into blossoms,

into a glimmer of green, shimmer of dew washing our toes.
Bathing us in a song that splits open a space for something that
might eclipse the sorrow

for beauty, for a pocket that might carry the things we can no
longer hold. We release a stone of heaviness as our limbs move
and sway, stretch and swirl

like the leaves, bound together by their branches but free —
free to seep in the light, the song lifting us into the jazz blue
sun-soaked Louisiana sky.

Janet Fagal

Tea for All the Broken Places

Her porch so inviting
designed almost Gatsby-like,
whispers *welcome*.
Soft tones muted like our friendship,
drift toward the sidewalk.
Bright colors: orange, turquoise, yellow, spell warmth.
They belie winter's approach.
We will soon be pummeled by snowstorms.
Subtle whimsy abounds.
Here a metal rooster, there
a round green pitcher
brimming with blue hydrangea.
You wonder how you could have stayed away so long?
Smiles mingle with conversation and forgiveness.
Finally broken no more you visit.
Years of yearning evaporate.
Her musings a balm.
Hot tea slips through your cracks.
She offers insight and hope.
Her husband's Parkinson's? Not a trouble,
only one more thing to cradle with love.
The toasted apple muffin she offers, so buttery and warm,
wraps your heart in richest pops of red.

Beach Music

My young mother knew beach life.
The draw to salt-fed air
mixed forever in her blood.
At birth she spilled sea fever into mine.
That potion a spirit-salve
found in sunlit simplicity and salt water.

In girlhood she knew summers
living camp-style at water's edge;
sunny beach days without care bayside.
Rowing, reading, digging clams.
Oceanside, she'd jump gentle waves,
race the undertow, collect shells.
She knew turbulent times.
Dark sea days, seething with ocean's anger.
Winds howling a raging screed.

On holiday I sit staring out at my past.
The horizon of my childhood golden,
festooned with sundrenched days by the sea;
sand a second skin,
the breeze a welcome balm,
my mother's lessons as steady as wave music.

For a moment I return
to the lighthouse of my mother's embrace,
the windmill, the cliffs,
clam pie and picnics.
In glittering light my mother,
 young once more, sparkles.
Her love then as sure as the heart-shaped driftwood I finger.

On rare beach days I recall these long ago moments.
A reminder of darkness and light,
this music of the sea,
clear as the water I watch.
Coming in, going out.

Deborah Filanowski

Maybe I Can Start with a Tattoo

Music rose louder, beat against me,
drinks flowed, laughter, more raucous.
The room in the old church hall
turned community center,
turned into pop-up drag show,
thrummed with excited voices.
Queens strutted their stuff
to 'Uptown Funk' and 'New York, New York'
as cheering boozy patrons
stuffed dollar bills into hands and bras.
Like the lowly, work-a-day caterpillar
the queens turned the drab
commonness of everyday living into butterfly beauty,
turned the mundane into high drama
as they emerged from their own cocoons,
heightening the already charged atmosphere.
And I chortled, thinking of the church forefathers
and their perceptions of sacred.
Freedom was in the air,
causing a ripple of sadness in my own cosmos
thinking about society's constraints,
wearing the skin you are given
expectations based on gender.
Little girls don't, women don't,
just fill in the blank.
Wearing a tiara and Spanx won't change me now
and I am not interested in being a hyper queen.
Let me break free from this chrysalis of society's making,
let my soul shine, stretch its wings, prepare to fly.
Is it too late to change into something new,
or must I wait for my next life?
Tonight, I leave energized and
upbeat, witness to a renaissance of sorts,
rejoicing that some people have escaped earth's bounds.

All Good Fairy Tales End in Blood

By all means,
read fairy tales to your daughters,
entice them to believe all stories begin
with "once upon a time" and
end with "happily ever after."
Promote the perpetual image of the pure
radiant, virgin, unsoiled, unspoiled,
but no matter,
danger waits behind each door,
stalks the innocent,
be it the manticore ready to pounce
or the old, fat, rich man
seeking a child bride to warm
his bed and pledge her troth.
Pay off the family to seal the bargain
gain access to the treasure,
but there is only one prize
in a box of Cracker Jacks
and age eats youth
even if the mirror lies for a time
until it can lie no more.
But karma is a bitch,
all good fairy tales end in blood,
how else to satisfy the gods?
Good, rewarded,
evil, punished,
so the story goes.
Queen Clementianna dances to her death
in iron shoes heated in the forge
at Snow White's wedding feast;
Cinderella's wicked stepmother is
bound to four horses sent to the Cardinal points;
Mother Gothel starves in the lonely tower
she crafted for Rapunzel.
Do not think the story over,
not all the truth is evident.
The virgin also bleeds,
first in the marriage bed,
then at the birth of every baby
to please the heir-hungry Prince,
now ruler of the kingdom.
There is seldom a happy ending,

kings not always faithful,
some mother-in-laws still want to be Queen,
keep the crown and the family jewels.
Read deep,
do not count on the fairy tale for comfort,
better to arm your tender virgins with swords,
teach them martial arts,
a livable skill, and send them out into
the world to make their own way.

In Whom Can We Trust?

Sex is not a personal matter,
never a private issue between consenting adults,
the act and its consequences regulated by laws and mores,
politics and social constructs.
Sequestered from the human condition,
the patriarchs, fathers of us all, sit, with fat bellies and swollen egos
in state houses around the country deciding what is best for women
they will never meet,
determining the fate of babies they will never feed.
The Pharisees sit in judgment of all women
proscribing what they may and may not
do with their bodies according to their holier-than-thou wisdom.
Every woman offered up as sacrifice,
every baby and child, a pawn in this game of control.
These wise men will not vote for a livable wage,
will not strike guns from the hands of abusers,
will not raise up each child to an equitable standard.
As employees of the people, they vote themselves raises,
mistake wealth for wisdom, power and privilege for sanctity.
Their words are honeyed even as they drip venom.
These leaders drink good whiskey, laugh at each other's
dirty jokes, pleased to be "just one of the boys,"
slap each other on the back for a good job done,
while children in this great nation go to bed at night hungry.
Never wanting you to know that the power resides in you,
not in their pomp and puppetry,
In your vote, in your support.
It is not about political parties,
it is about being human and caring about each other
that is our godliness and our humanity.

Mary Gardner

Between Times

"Sleep such as makes the darkness brief..."
yearns Martial, soldier of ancient Rome
with no last name,

his words flowing over me
as I turn thin pages of what remains
in collected works and possible quotes,
something I will toss into a discard bin
after one last scan
for penciled notes and post-its—
hints of what mattered back then.

Small comfort it seems, even now,
to let sleep ransom the coming day,
the healing power of fading grief.
I have aged. You have not.
Requiescat in pace.

On the Issue of Provenance

Have you considered the provenance of a poem—
how it came to be, what inspired its unfolding
across the page, when its journey is complete?

Is a poem not nurtured in invention summoned
from what we have lived or mused upon or left
in the barely conscious? Or learned and applied
from the work of noted poets, past and present?

And does not the discovery itself enliven
the quest, whatever the choices one employs
in the poem's subsequent telling?

As one given to unfettered reads and re-writes,
first to myself and later with colleagues,
am I not thus gifted with new insights, options,
perhaps a re-visioning of the truth I seek to tell?

Having given these questions due consideration,
and certainty being a matter of choice,
I cannot say a poem is mine
except to own the effort.

The GREAT TSUNAMI December 26, 2004
Twelve Nations, One Story

At The Seaside

When I was down by the sea
A wooden spade they gave to me
To dig the sandy shore.

My holes were empty like a cup.
In every hole the sea came up
Till it could come no more.

                              ~Robert Louis Stevenson

I

It was morning under a bright blue sky—

children digging deep holes in the sand
searching for the bottom of the world,
the other side of the earth;

beyond the beach, a lagoon and skiffs lying adrift,
hanging baskets, skirts and beads to charm the eye,
breakfast alfresco under shaded pergolas and shanty roofs,
wind chimes and rustling fronds, petals touching down.

II

Gone, that morning under a bright blue sky
when the sea exploded up from its dungeon six miles below;
when the earth quaked to Magnitude 9 and split open its crust
of heaving plates, jolting two seconds off the clock forever;
when the earth sucked up the edges of the sea
and sent them back as though unleashed.
                    This, the Great Tsunami
racing five hundred miles an hour, continent to continent,
tall walls of sea smothering everything in its wake, villages
crashing and dropping wherever the waters left them.
Noah's cries rose above the roar.

III

Just as suddenly, the waters drew back, leaving
landscapes broken and littered, train on its side,
mosque left standing, stone Buddha sitting properly.

Hundreds of thousands of people
were erased from the living and found
in tidal swells and rubble, the Wall of Faces.
Survivors wandered, dazed, the real and unreal
blurring in a welcome respite from haunting memory.

Helicopters whirred overhead, cameras on story,
alerting a responsive world.

IV

Evening settled down in the silence,
an arc of sun passing below the horizon.
The sea lay tranquil as though nothing had happened.
One lone tree, robbed of full bloom, quivered
on a rise above the shore. Under it,
a monk was sitting, eyes closed,
praying.

Caitlin Gemmell

Bloodlines

Last night I dreamed of Grandmere
whose hands never crinkled like wadded crepe paper.
They were smooth as milk and just as giving.
Offered from the palm of her hand were tiny gifts
such as butterscotch, ladybugs, and dandelions
we would wish on and whose seeds would scatter
in all directions. It's comforting how family rituals
are invisible threads, weaving us together,
as my mother, whose hands are a topographical map,
gives my child a bouquet of leaves of maple he delights
in arranging on his personal altar much as I once
curated treasures from my own grandmother.

In Memory of Seven Hens

April of another spring and earlier than usual
the lilacs are budding, their scent on the cusp
of nearly intoxicating. The dandelions we gathered
(in the rain as one does) are sizzling in a puddle of butter.
Popping one into my mouth, the tears come
not because they are too hot nor for their delectable,
savory taste.
Instead, I'm reminded of our last life and our seven hens,
each of them with their own cravings
but united in their love of fritters
of the dandelion variety,
similar to the bittersweet buds I can no longer eat
without wondering where the taste of salt comes from.
Salt and tears, both are reminders
of a seaside cottage and seven hens we miss daily.

Carol Lynn Stevenson Grellas

Trying to Remember the Unforgettable

What you can't remember is why
on that morning, your father had a gun
when your mother said *come
quick, we need to leave the house*—

if he was after you or himself,
or a beast that lived within him
as if somehow you never
knew the difference.

What you can't remember is what
day it was or why you wore your
yellow nightgown, the one with
daisies handstitched around

the collar and little puffed sleeves
as you hurried through your grandmother's
garden, past rows of pink chrysanthemums
that seemed to bloom in arrogance

while you scurried along sidewalks, parked
cars, neighbors sitting in their yards,
your mother yanking at you like a hound
on a leash—angrily, no, forcefully, no, afraid.

What you can't remember is
how long he's been gone now, if
it's been years that seem like minutes
or minutes that seem like years

or why, when you read about his
death in the paper, the word suicide
is still a surprise, even all these
years— yet still, you lay down

on the grass and hear the hum
of his voice in the trees, his shadow
rustling through leaves, and the sound
of his rifle, loaded and cocked.

Elizabeth Hayhoe

Rose Coloured Glasses

the same rose coloured glasses
that skewed my vision of you
turned everything we built red
burning red, setting ablaze my own skin
until I'm left with only ashes
but I am no phoenix, I will not rise from the dead
and you killed me
you threw away the key
that led to the reasons for my love
you did not deserve the words I wrote
under the false pretence
of the rose coloured glasses
yet they are now yours forever
to have and to hold, unlike me
because I was never yours to keep
like a wilted flower dying of thirst
you kept me on display for far too
long unable to think through the haze
you truly believed I'd survive the storm
but a cut flower will only die, petals falling to the floor
as I did
for, my love, you were the death of me
when you gave the little love I thought I deserved
the smoke blown in my face
the rose coloured glasses made it appear as magic
I accepted the love you had to give
although it would never be enough
it wasn't written in stone
only on the inside of the rose coloured glasses
and taking them off was one of the hardest things
I'd ever done
in a moment I'd long to put the glasses back
but they'd no longer fit my face
as I faced reality
that the pretty pink skies I had, were a bleak grey
rose lens could no longer skew my perspective
as I looked you clearly in the eye

and ended it between us
though you had ended me long ago
through torments and belittlement
you killed me slow, that girl will never come back
she will simply sit in the ash of a home you burned.

John Herington

Paper Pretzels

She offered me pretzels
on the plane to Milan
as I gazed below
at the white snow
a rice-paper thin
20,000 feet thin
while in the carriage beyond
played the paper-hat boys
destined for fun -
then I remembered
I'd eaten those pretzels
and only the paper
the paper plane
of my dreams
was keeping me high
and helping me fly

Apotheosis

Before the rain comes
I would dance on roses
and sleep on a pin
watch a crow chase a duck
and count ripples on water
walk 'holloways'
and cycleways
and mountainways
to find sunsets
but now I look for Acers
in the garden and
the Gingbo tree
to feed my soul—
before the rain comes

Lindsey Jacobs

How to Write a Poem in Ten Steps

Step one
Grab the black sequined journal and hot pink feathered pen you bought with the very last of your birthday money. Trace your fingers over the messy scrawl of your name on the inside cover and grimace at the scratch of sequins against your bare legs.

Step two
Flip to a blank page and write. Write about the dreams and memories that won't leave you alone. Write and write and write until your emotions are a pit of vitriol and you've run out of ink.

Step three
Reach into your chest and rip out your heart. Dip into the inkwells of its arteries and use your blood and angst as ink, scream out your soul into a diary entry so devastating it leaves you breathless and gasping for hours.

Step four
Bury it in a diary, in a box, in the very back of your closet. Bury it under winter coats, old yearbooks and the Halloween costume you wore when you were three. Bury it so deep even you forget it's there.

Step five
Ten years later on a cold January afternoon in a desperate hunt for a lost stocking cap, unearth your rotting heart.

Step six
Let your eyes explore the cancerous growth of your childhood. Run your fingers over every vein to read its Braille and let each heartbeat tell your story in Morse code.

Step seven
Read it to your mother. Each sentence escaping in a stuttering scorching screech. Watch as she winces and whimpers away from your vulnerability. The pain in each word still so piping hot and viscous they burn your throat and her skin on the way out. The heat will leave you both raw and squirming for days.

Step eight
Edit and edit and edit until your bared soul is disfigured and dripping in metaphor. Until a reader can take what they need from it, and you can read it without weeping. This version will be palatable, but it will not be your story. There will be no catharsis in its creation, no healing in its wholeness.

Step nine
Call your therapist.

Step ten
Write a new verse. Title it "an ode to my 13-year-old self". Apologize for burying her in the closet, for stifling her sonnets between rule line pages. Thank her for her bravery, let her know she is safe now. Urge her to keep writing because one day she will be able to write a poem that doesn't feel like a gaping wound were her heart once was. One day she will write a poem that heals more than it hurts, one day she will write a poem in ten steps.

A Body is Water

Every body is an ocean.
Mine an estuary,
where salt and fresh water meet.
My heart a tide pool,
I can always find you there.
Listening to the waves,
crash and break,
freedom in their foamy flow.
Can you feel the current?
The rip tides grip,
pulling us under.
Saltwaters sweet sting,
Oceans' kiss.
Algae covered emotions ebb,
revealing the expanse between us.
My buoyed hope,
kept under loch and key.
What is a baby other than a small stream formed from a bigger body.
Birth a briny baptism.

Daedalus Grieves

Released from that lowering labyrinth.
Freedom of flight blesses you fledgling.
Stretch your scrunched wings.
But I caution you,
"Fly between the extremes."

As you fell so did my heart.
Swallowed by the ocean.
Body barren.
Feathers floating.
My only son washed ashore.

Who is to blame?
Do I dare curse the sun god or king of the seas?
It was your hubris.
But did I not raise you?
Teach you?
Handcraft and handover the very tool of your demise.

I now lay my wings at Apollo's feet.
For the gift of flight, I am undeserving.
I beg of you patron of Delphi,
In this temple I built in your honor,
One grieving father of foolish son to another.
Bless my child's journey,
flying high enough to touch the heavens.
May he reach Elysium at last.

As I travel out from Crete,
I am sound in the knowledge I will not build again.
Skilled hands, cursed work.
Architect of great prestige
My greatest creation,
Was you.

Jennifer Maloney

Dear Orgasm,

How lucky I am to have known you.
Friends for fifty-five years now, you and I,
and still, every time we meet,
a pleasure.
Who else can claim that kind of record?

Not that we haven't had our differences.
I would have preferred that you'd come
unencumbered
with needs, the way you did
when we both were younger:

dropping by unexpectedly
the first time I biked
down the rocky slide
of the gully at the end of Galena Street,
or the days we lay pressed against
the living room carpet,
Dark Shadows on the tube,
the vampire's teeth bared, barely stroking
the upturned underside
of a long, willing throat—
the fun, the fear, the fantasy!
We held each other's hands,
and played together nicely.

At first, you didn't like my boyfriends.
Never wanted to be introduced.
But when Danny DeWine rolled up
on his new Yamaha—a crotch-rocket
that buzzed and sizzled like a hornet
underneath my thighs—oh, then
you were all dreamy sighs,
you adorable slut.
At least until he sold it to my brother.

But these days,
you decline invitations for weeks at a time.

Too tired, a backache, another surgery.
Excuses, excuses—
well, excuse me, but I have a date tonight
with a sweet little ride I've known for years—
known to buzz, and sometimes sizzle—
with a smile full of sharp little canines,
perfectly willing to bite.

Please, don't fight me on this.
Come see me.

I'll make all the preparations, dear,
you won't have to do a thing—
just show up, stand up, take a bow.
I know you haven't practiced,
but you're the star of this show—

the supple neck of the swooning starlet,
the hypnotic gaze, the swirl of the cape—
and I'm happy to stand offstage,
behind the curtain, directing the action,
feeding you lines until
muscle memory takes over,
when you'll suddenly remember
how
the story
goes.

Glass

Two jobs and a side hustle, and this
is what I can afford, sighs my friend,
gesturing at her four new walls,
*A studio apartment. A **studio**.*
With my teenager.

At least the room is pretty big, she says,
standing in the middle of the pretty big room,
empty but for a radiator that bangs
and bubbles beneath the windows.
Elbows of plumbing shinny the walls
and ceiling, everything babyshit brown,
lumps of dried paint-drips sprouting
like mushrooms. A tiny stove, sink,
and refrigerator squat in the corner,
six inches of counterspace
wedged, like a grudge, between.
The windows are big, too, she says,
they let in lots of light,
and doesn't remark
how they rattle in their frames
each time a semi drives by.
I know I'm lucky, she murmurs,
a smile struggling, the corners of her eyes
squeezed, wrung out like dishrags.
This is lucky.

There are people, I have read—
Charles VI of France is one—
who develop the odd delusion
that they are made of glass.
Normal in other respects,
they are constantly anxious
about their fragile state, frightened
that they might shatter. A psychiatrist
once questioned such a patient, asking
what *the feeling of being made of glass*
meant to him, so the patient asked the doctor
to look out the window, describe what he saw.
He saw the street, he said: cars, other buildings,
people passing by, and the patient replied,

Ah! You've missed the glass in the window.
You didn't see it. But it is there.

The next thing we say to each other,
here, in this pretty big studio, this new home
my friend is trying to make with her child—
burned-out bulbs and roach-bait stink,
clanks and hisses, vibrates, shakes the way

a good wife oughta shake,
rattling those pots and pans, shakes
like a dry martini, like a stripper's ass,

like a frightened dog or a cowering boy,
or a hand flung up to ward off a blow—

the next thing that I say will matter,
though not as much
as the things that shatter a world,
somehow imperceptible as glass.
They are there, but we don't see them,
we only notice when they break,
so I say *It's beautiful, Honey, beautiful.*
I think you'll be happy here.

Unspeakable

How unlucky to be this way,
to be able to map this adventure,
this life, only with words.
Words forsake us too soon;
one comes to a point
where the color is the only thing
that will speak its own name,
and the shape, the only trail to follow.

There is nothing to be said,
no way I can tell you
what the garden sings to me
in its scents, the poems written
on petals that wither and drop,
rot sweetly into warm earth,
create a bed, a cradle,
for something new.

How can I describe a green
that feels thirsty? That stretches,
lifts its head, opens its mouth
like a palm to cup the raindrops,
receive the communion of water?
Whose speech patters down around me,
exclaims! in large, wet plops,
or rivers down the black top drive,
writing a manuscript
that I can never read?

The small sounds that fall from my lips
are finite, stony boxes. Nothing can enter
or enlarge them, they are a void,
no light escapes them,

but the language of pebbles
is, in fact, music,
and will open to water,
break down, become sand,
allow itself to be transported
through the air, hanging in the wind,
scrawling stories over mountain tops,

against white cliffs, then slide
into the ocean to inform it,
in its silvery speech,
whisper secrets into the ears
of fish and mermaids,
who listen, nod, then lift
a conch shell to their lips,
and gossip what was told to them
by sand, salt, and water.

The words I have for this miracle
can tell you nothing.
Words can only follow that path,
not communicate it.
To understand it at all,
I think we must stop speaking.
I think we must become still,

press our soft feet
and fingers
into this generous world,
who wants to tell us everything.
Who wants us
to listen.

Katherine Meadows

Compendium of Sunlights

Spring
California burned and for a week,
all the sunlight touching down looked like spilled paint.
spilled the way that honey oozes from the living wax of honeycomb,
when its tiny enclosed chambers are gashed
in winter, when I return to such exposed comb,
its once warm cavities are feathery and fragile where I find them,
crumpled and cold, tucked into my chest
I keep trying to form circles perfectly using only my mind,
keep fires going between my fingers
and as spring blooms into the grey landscape,
I feel the dead ache of skeletal honeycomb
as it pulls the raw edges where living tissue of my ribcage meets
dying, meets dead.
the pull of the dead on this sore, living puncture coagulates
questions in the greening atmosphere—
of the memories contained in hollow comb
once festering with brood and fermenting nectar
and the distilled honey of flox, locust, solidago and a hillside
of asters, ignited in new spring's ethereal golden sunlight

Summer
I burn to transmute my want into need
I burn intoxication addiction for reprieve
I burn last season's hay to disturb the pumping alarm hormones of bees
I burn to separate the stinger from the sting

The smoke from California drifts across the continent,
intersecting with the sunlight I drive through
turning the whole day into golden hour
and I ask if it's okay that

People will be stung by summer kisses
as long as their hunger pulls them onto steaming roads
That coronets of hornets will crown us
with interminable questions,
That incinerated earth can be so beautiful,
 a thousand miles from its source.

This sinking portal of the sun that touches down

and brings me to shards
Charring trees, baking the clay and rock into deserted comb,
a hollowed home only for hungry bees
Flaming pottery of my flesh,
wraps arms around a buzzing fantasy
that suffuses me, unshingling as it goes.
I cannot hold helium sun:
Hung from above, makes me feel myself as crockery—
Feeble arms straining up to be held, to claw closer,
tearing the mask off a torrent of

nothing, only smoke
that I begged to be water.
A death instinct dribbles off my parched lips
howls through hollows in the concave sternum and sacrum
billows from my nostrils
through fiber glass lungs.
It might as well be an ember

When you're driving on the road with an urgent sense of direction,
but the road starts to get very
steep until it bends straight up like a harmonica's brass expansion.
And you proceed with side glances that ask "is this alright?"
honey hanging from your eyes.
You think you just felt your rear wheels dangle and bounce
for a moment.
August storms swarm in your heart,
nectar collecting in your ribcage, stopping up alveoli.
And the road keeps inclining.

it is suggested you may turn upside down
vigilantly, I watch the faces for you, or thunderstorms
as I trace worn circles around moonlit backroads
when it's a perfect circle, eternity can fit into it
until then I blow smoke rings from my incendiary chest

There are two sides to the road and the middle is not one of them.
I'm driving on a black night road, being only ignited by passers.

On the map it's a straight line and I slide along curves
I'm only following without my bearings
I keep coming home from a death instinct
I keep stockpiling spoons

It's coming off a week's end in the ellipse of some arms,
washing the smell off my sheets.
It's remembering that sad is a name I wear.

It's the possibility that all questions are answerable
—all hinging like orgasm from the heavy clouds bent on rain.
I had to wash my body in womb blood under a full moon
to unprickle my flesh.
To invite green spring into my singed center

Autumn
In the sun-reddened water
they go on indefinitely, deciding to love and to not.

What story do the bees experience? They just exist.
That's it, and that's not the point.

I remember everything that flew over the water
and touched down on my surface like a passing riptide.

Sunlight will catch bees
and drizzle with golden attachment across our hearts,
Will drive us off a well-lit road,
till we need the blind night to finally surrender:
Open the mouth to vomit questions,
and exhale months of smoke

And you feel it burn your skin.
All that living air
seems to suggest the burning honeycomb of my anatomy
is a temporary answer.

Yellow falls off the sun
and slides down the long fingers of trees.

I don't have to watch the windows for cars.
I know this without turning myself around
in the corner and watching the sunset in light

That dims across the kitchen floor,
collecting in puddles around my house.

Nicole Metts

Passing

I cannot touch what has left.
Each breath the better.
Until there is no other.

I know.
Children never forget.
Not sure about god.
Enveloped.
Stuck in the sky.
An old man reading.
His book.
From a light house.

A remembrance.
Rouses him.
Not a breath.
A nonbreath.
The wind blows.
A lost garden.
Children never forget.
And remain.
Searching.

A Mother Wars

I gave you the moon of my body to first sail the world.
How easy it is to love a stranger, as you grew,
A blossom that knows only the pull of the universe.

When you fell out of the sky, the moon lit the grass.
You cried the sorrow of losing something,
Something I wish I could remember.

You floated into my arms, your ancient eyes of ocean
Taking in the light between us.
I gave you the river of my body. Then watched you dream

Under the waning moon. Your father curled beside us.
Time stopped, then jumped.
Until the impatient ticking woke the moon in you.

The moon, in a river, the river going to the ocean,
An ocean deep and dark and endless,
This I cannot stop.

All I can do is show you the light to come back to.

Ophelia

"Too much of water hast thou, poor Ophelia, And therefore I forbid my tears" -Shakespeare

Twilight burned the sky, even the water was aflame, in madness, heartbroken madness, and daisies and dead man's fingers, pale woven garland, I know why the willow weeps and touches the current softly singing, bent down into the deep depths of swollen pool that once a siren claimed wrapped in garments that caressed her body and pulled like the sails of a ship; periwinkles and buttercups floated from her golden locks and followed as if a dream, or a goddess. There is nothing like a lover's cry of loss as her lips shall never kiss, and her hysteria becomes his as they lay the senseless girl and her wildflowers in her grave where the willow roots and her virtue stays entombed.
But is not love a kind of madness you fall helpless into?

Kate Potter

Out There
   for Michael (1953 – 2024)

wind is barely moving
even so, boughs of the pine are waving
gently
at the sky

even as you stirred the world
moved it
gently
with purpose, always with purpose
colossal
your spirit – large
made its way into our hearts
with steadfast defiance

boughs of the pine are waving
a gentle dance

gentle as your going
with the wind
not down into nothingness

boughs of the pine are still waving

your faint goodbye
a promise
till another day

Nursing Home

When I first moved in
I asked my aide had anyone ever died in this bed
Someone's died in all these beds, she said
It's a nursing home.

Mohammed Shohidur Rahman

The Spider's Love For Cheryl

I have lain this simple note by the fine nook of your ear,
Cheryl, as you lay sleeping,
Perplexed by your grievous case of epilepsy. Wriggling grubs
and evil lice have wended
Their way into your temple, and a most cavalier caterpillar is
entertaining his noisome tribe
With tales regaled by the spiral of your cochlea.
The pink sac of a baby rat is somewhere hanging like an
ampoule, while
In the moonlight its mum and dad roll tumbrils of syrup and
dirt to make their nest.
All the while the lattice of the moon has created a luminous
thread for the golden spider to work,
And an owl is hooting gently that the hour is getting late and
the world must be to bed.
I too must sleep, but since I've had fifteen minutes to spare,
I used it to write to you.

Mark this — though I've embellished this sheet with relish,
adorned it with music,
And mended my broken charactering — words and spells
pulled out of the air
To hang like cobwebs — ghostly as the flea, they settle,
induced by
Chemicals or sorcery, making transference of zany electric
impulse —
That they may strike of little consequence to you — this is true —
But to me — ah, my dear sparrow! — all my heart I have
poured forth,
A rushing spring's bouquet drank in the pining, lilac neck of
autumn.
A wicker basket is now full of carnations, a glass vase full
of tulips.
This is my card whereon is writ my devotion.

Take note, my petal, that the North wind soon shall blow,
And in winter's dull grip a drift of snow shall before time close
my door to you.

Then, even old Uranus' song shall be in vain and he'll put
up his harp,
And wandering beyond Kuiper's belt, lose teeth, lose potency,
lose belief.

Could you bid Cheryl be in a trance? Or comb her yellow hair?
    Could you bid her lids be set with pearls? Look, the purple
of the Aegean is in her eyes.
From aquamarine and topaz she shall be cast. Or otherwise
shall be engraved in shell,
    Set as a glittering pendant to be worn by two-penny bit sham
divines.
Rather let her be suspended in time, and let me, fluttering overhead,
    Never descending, never giving in, utter instead something
inspired of harmony,
More vexed and roaring than when the full moon tides and
sucks in half the world.

    Well might I have held Cheryl's snowy hand in mine. — Not
even Jade Emperors could have
    Worn her mitt as fit for theirs' — made of such an ermine,
yet as ordinary as millet.
Bring on oils in her absence, bring on nuptials,
    Bring on variegated aromas in vials plentiful, and viands
ambrosial,
Play on a soothing sarabande if you must.
    O why not bring on the gorgeous, unfurling wing of the Im-
perial butterfly then,
You gods who've decided these things, if you cannot bring her
to me?

    But never bid me to know of my lady's parting from hence,
Nor let old age graze her hair to make it aspen.
    Aye, yonder lies my angel of epileptic fury shaking. —
None could be so proud
As my tender Cheryl, soft as the lips of dawn, as strong as a bar
of iron.

Lynne Schmidt

When I Run Out of Things To Talk About, I Talk About Horses

On her birthday, I show my aunt photos of Charlie,
the white unicorn I've been taking lessons on for over a year.
I tell her I am not good yet,
I am still learning how to trot,
and I'm bad at keeping my feet in the right places.

At her deathbed,
I tell her about the time he spooked,
and threw me forward but I stayed on,
even when my instructor thought to herself,
"Today is the day she goes down!"

I tell her I broke my thumb nail,
show her photos of the split in the middle
and small bit of blood.

At her deathbed,
I run out of things to say.

And so I tell her how since the cold came,
Charlie has been spicy and I have to slow him down,
and the hardest part is keeping my feet still.

I tell her last Friday, Charlie forgot he has front legs,
and pitched forward.
How my instructor hollered, "And -that's- why you stay upright!"

I tell my aunt,
I did not fall off.

The Wedding Ring

I sit with my dead aunt's body for nearly two hours.

When people talk about being haunted,
I wonder if what they mean is the absence of breath
after focusing on it for the last six hours.

I wonder if they mean the way
the fever takes twenty minutes
to leave the body.

I wonder if it's the way the nurse asks me
if I'd like to remove her rings,
or wait for the mortician.

At first, because I don't want to touch her
once all the warmth is gone,
I say I'll wait.

But as time moves forward,
as she becomes colder,
I worry her fingers will swell.

I worry if I don't do it now,
they will have to break her fingers
to get them off.

I wonder when people talk about being haunted,
if it's the way
I removed her wedding ring,
from her cold, stiff, hand.

How there was one ring left,
I could not slide off.

How now when I see a person wearing a ring,
I wonder who will be the one to remove it.

Peggy Seely

Home

Home is a cardboard box under a bridge on the Lower East Side
I divide my sandwich from the dumpster with Larry the Rat
You think he's a guy I know used to be in the gang
No he's really a rat skinny like me we huddle when it's cold

See Larry and me we're birds of a feather two of a kind
Brothers from another mother like they say nowadays. Mother.
Oh momma she'd hum me to sleep tell me the Sandman's comin'
Gonna put sleepy dust in my eyes Gonna make everything all better

Home was a little farm upstate with chickens and a cow
A sway-backed old horse name of Duke two rescued puppies
The old man scooped from a ditch before he gave up and left
Then home was over a saloon in Brooklyn with my funny uncle

Barracks in Jersey felt like home at seventeen Gonna make things
All better but home was a hospital to fight pneumonia before home
Was a foxhole in Kuwait and that's where the Sandman hit me
With his sleepy dust Oh Momma

Somebody said old age comes on suddenly I'm 53 I'm old momma
Older than dirt older than God older than I should be. Kids run by
Jeering, kick dirt in my face. Larry and me we say fuck you friends
We're home

Spacebar Skips

Thank you, Time's Up Movement

Remington, Royal, Smith-Corona Museum
pieces now. I helped build them test-typist
my title. After semi-final before the case
was installed

Wind the ribbon all the way to the end
wind it back the other way
Is it smooth? Does the auto-reverse engage?
Strike each key for sticking, all 47

Check shift keys, shift lock, carriage lock tab
set/clear, margin set/clear, color selector (only
if you have black/red ribbon useful
in certain businesses) margins and backspace

Remember the ratchet release lever. Type the test
paragraph over and over and over. You see in
your sleep the quick brown fox jumping over the
lazy dog 1234567890

Smile when the manager comes by, stops to
breathe in your ear. Hi cutie, would ya for a
big red apple? Ignore the dolt on his
way to the men's room who unfailingly chortles

Wanna kiss your uncle good-bye before
I shake the piss outta him? Keep your cool
when you return a machine to a semi-final inspector
because the spacebar skips. Don't lean over it
he sneers. It's your big boobs making that happen

Comforter

Each morning I smooth it across my bed
scattered bouquets in pastels its design.
For accent, I toss pillows: aqua, lavender, coral. It's
feminine. I'm free to do that now.

I bought it a few months ago at a thrift shop;
first in line when it opened that morning, there
to snag costume paraphernalia
for my Amateur Theater Group.

As I dashed past the bedding section, it caught my
eye; I grabbed it. A few minutes later
a girl, twelve or so, made for the bin, turned to her
mom with a stricken look, spotted me.

They obviously knew what they wanted waited
for half-price day, got there as soon
as the bus could take them, my sporty red car
unfair competition. I felt her trail me.

Absorbed her hope. Aware of her shabby shoes
unstylish outfit, avoiding her doe eyes, I shopped. I
saw the little purse she clutched, fat with dollar bills I
bet she spent a long time saving.

I could have ordered a comforter like it from
Amazon, paid the thrift price five times over.
I could have strolled back to the bedding bin
making sure she was close behind, made a show

of looking it over, shaking it out, holding it to
the light, then placed it back in the bin relishing
the joy in her face. I could have. Each morning
as I smooth it across my bed
I think: Why didn't I?

Kathleen Strafford

Family Reunion

Down a long mud-red lane with pits and rocks
to celebrate my great grandfather's birthday

After the feast the women's skirts swept high
as they gathered up their home-spun dishes
                                        chittering away
The men with cigars and braces clinked bottles of bathtub beer

I found my way down a hidden pathway to a gate to gaze into a field
where a hierarchy of flowers and a meandering creek beckoned
                                        with small wiggly minnows

Uncle Bill said   *don't turn around*
A bull thinks he owns the field, if you go there he'll chase you

His chin whiskers combed through my blonde curls
He whispered how he wanted to find it
as his finger slipped down my pedal pushers
the green grass and wild flowers turned grey as the barn
The silken label on my panties read
                        Pretty girls Sail into Spring

On the Farm with the Warren Boys

Without a thought for danger
we rolled & hid in the hayloft squishing spiders
bounced on the back of the tractor
hanging off wheels diving into deep pit holes.
                            touched electric fences
squirted milk from udders at cats mewling in the corner
            as dogs chased squirrels in wet-nosed yards

And to fatten our joy, the boys said, *let's gig for frogs*!
Without a clue I grabbed a stick with spikes
We searched through widow's weeds
stomped on snails laughing at the crunch
Rabbits high-tailed away in waterfalls of sunshine
                            clouds hovering over the roofs

The creek was full of hoppy toads, crawdads and tadpoles
                    minding their own business

The boys stood like savages, feet balanced,
spears high and straight
                hearts became swinging bricks, *Lord of the Flies*
                    with a look that would drown kittens.
Crawdads were waving their pincers
singing frogs   screamed as tines plunged into green bellies.
Terror cattle-prodded me.   I yelled threw my stick and ran

crying to their mom, she said   *Boys must learn how to act*
tough   be strong like men
                she walked with me
                    to pick bouquets of delicate Queen Anne's Lace
                        wedding gowns for song birds and starlings

Bill Tope

I Have Dreams, Too

I am disabled,
trapped in a shell
that doesn't
always do what
I tell it to.
But I'm not that
different from
you.

I have dreams,
in living color,
and, like
everyone, I
enjoy the
fragrance of
spring flowers,
the scent of new
mown grass and
freshly turned
earth and coffee.

I crave
companionship
as much as
you do, and I
want to share
my life and
thoughts with
another Just like
you do.

I enjoy sweet
strawberry
jam and ice
tinkling in my
glass of tea.

I like the feel of
sand between my
toes at the beach,

the crunch of fallen
leaves beneath
my boots in the
forest.

I need the touch
of another's hand
in my own. Their
lips upon my brow.

Though I may
seem distracted or
muddled or even
confused, that does
not mean I'm not
aware; that I don't
see the smirks or
the eye rolls or
the other gestures
of impatience or
intolerance from
others

You see, I have
dreams, too.

Luke Williams

The Extra Mile

Alarm!
First warning—
    Brushes away
the suggestion that he needs help.

Pants … laboured breathing
Booted. Pulls socks up.

Get cracking!

Belts out
        Primordial scream
Loud
"You can do this!"

Tie in a knot
Jacket … straight.
Pins fastened
To secure his climb up that corporate cliff.

Today he will not make his
Bread and butter—but will

Drive
    himself
        mad
            Along the highway of the corridor,
racing through the red lights
to get ahead -
splintering the sunroof -

a Stain on his record.

Who said something about a bloody glass ceiling?

Diana Woodcock

To Live in the Grace of Gaia

Considering how to live
in the grace of Gaia,
I would follow in the foot-

steps of the gentle people
of Tibet, that third pole,
land of snows from which

the greatest source of water flows.
Who lives more fully
together with wildness

than Tibetan nomads with their yaks?
Enter the enemy, the invader
forcing nomads into settlement shacks,

stripping the mountains of resources
damming the rivers. Enter
political terror, violence,

the CCP. Considering how to
live in the Great Mother's grace,
I trace the terrors and denials,

how we mask with smiles
the truths about wars and empires,
the instigators and facilitators,

social and spiritual ruin,
the chaos of desire for money
and power. Considering

how to live in Gaia's grace,
I turn my face toward the sun
and sign up for Tantric tango

lessons, letting go my ego so
my seven chakras might ignite
with divine energy as I leave behind

the mind, *the government of intellect** --
everything but body and soul to live
          in the grace of Gaia.

Velimir Khlebnikov, from his his essay, "On Poetry"

71

Judges

Heidi Nightengale
Co-Owner/ Editor
Clare Songbirds Publishing House

Heidi has written for and published in local, regional and national literary magazines. She has written two volumes of poetry, *Bird Vision* (Pudding House) and *Tillable Soil* (Clare Songbirds) Heidi is retired from her faculty position at the State University of New York (SUNY) at Empire State College where she taught courses in writing, reading along with courses in human services. In addition to her poetry Heidi has written two children's books, *What Fragrance is the Moon?* and *Robert's Red Sweater*. She has been a writer in the schools for her work as a poet and children's writer in three states and over 80 preschool, elementary, middle and high school classrooms. She has also conducted local poetry workshops for the public at Cayuga Community College and the Finger Lakes Arts Council. She has been a featured reader of her poetry in libraries, bookstores and coffee house settings throughout Central New York for two decades.

Rachael Ikins
Poet & Associate Editor
Clare Songbirds Publishing House

Rachael Ikins is a graduate of Syracuse University and winner of the 2018 Independent Book Award for poetry for her collection *Just Two Girls*. She is a multiple prize-winning poet/novelist/artist having written seven chapbooks, a full-length poetry collection and a novel. Her artwork has hung from Cooperstown to the NYS Fair and in galleries from Albany to Syracuse and points between. Her favorite subject is the faces and eyes of animals. She lives in a small house with her animal family surrounded by nature and an enormous vegetable garden, fruits of which sustain her through winter. Besides drawing and writing, Rachael enjoys hiking with her dogs, biking on the lake, mushroom hunting and cooking. She is never without a book in hand.

Celest Woo
English Teacher
Trevor Day School, Manhattan

Celest has been a college professor at colleges in New York, New Jersey, and Colorado. She and has taught English as well as French. She has published a chapbook of poetry with Pudding House, and a full-length volume of poetry with Clare Songbirds. She has published scholarly work, as well as poetry, fiction, and memoir both online and in print. She is a modern dancer and choreographer, and is currently at work on a book-length memoir.

Sarah A. Etlinger
English Professor
Rock Valley College

Sarah is an English professor who lives in Milwaukee, Wisconsin, with her family. A *Pushcart* and *Best of the Net* nominee, she is the author of four books; most recently *A Bright Wound from* Cornerstone Press. Her work appears in *Rattle, Spoon River Poetry Review, Minyan Magazine, Pithead Chapel*, and many others. When not reading, writing, or teaching, she can be found cooking, baking, birdwatching, and spending time near Lake Michigan with her family.

Michael Sharp
Professor of English and Caribbean Studies

Michael Sharp was born in England and graduated from the Royal Conservatoire of Scotland and holds graduate degrees from universities in England and the United States. His doctorate is from the University of Wisconsin-Madison. He teaches English Literature and Caribbean Studies at the University of Puerto Rico in San Juan. Michael Sharp's poetry has been published on both sides of the Atlantic including two books of poetry, *The Dark Room* and Certain Silences (Clare Songbirds).